31.00

GRAPHIC PREHISTORIC ANIMALS
TERROR BIRD
PHORUSRHACOS

ILLUSTRATED BY ALESSANDRO POLUZZI

Smart Apple Media

Published by Smart Apple Media, an imprint of Black Rabbit Books
P.O. Box 3263, Mankato, Minnesota 56002
www.blackrabbitbooks.com

U.S. publication copyright © 2017 Smart Apple Media. International copyright reserved in all countries. No part of this book may be reproduced in any form without written permission from the publisher.

Produced by David West Children's Books
6 Princeton Court, 55 Felsham Road, London SW15 1AZ

Designed and written by Gary Jeffrey

Copyright © 2017 David West Children's Books

Library of Congress Cataloging-in-Publication Data

Names: Jeffrey, Gary, author. | Poluzzi, Alessandro, illustrator.
Title: Terror bird / written by Gary Jeffrey ; illustrated by Alessandro
   Poluzzi.
Description: Mankato, Minnesota : Smart Apple Media, [2017] | Series: Graphic prehistoric animals | Audience: K to grade 3._ | Includes index.
Identifiers: LCCN 2015036961| ISBN 9781625884138 (library binding) | ISBN 9781625884299 (ebook)
Subjects: LCSH: Phorusrhacos longissimus–Juvenile literature. | Phorusrhacos
   longissimus–Comic books, strips, etc. | Birds, Fossil–Juvenile
   literature. | Birds, Fossil–Comic books, strips, etc. | CYAC: Prehistoric
   animals. | LCGFT: Graphic novels.
Classification: LCC QE872.G8 W47 2017 | DDC 568.3–dc23
LC record available at http://lccn.loc.gov/2015036961

Printed in China
CPSIA compliance information: DWCB16CP
010116

9 8 7 6 5 4 3 2 1

CONTENTS

WHAT IS A TERROR BIRD?
Learn the facts about this amazing animal.

THE STORY...
TERROR BIRD IN THE JUNGLES OF SOUTH AMERICA
page 6

FOSSIL FINDS
Find out about terrifying terror birds' fossils.
page 22

ANIMAL GALLERY
Look up the animals that appear in the story.
page 23

GLOSSARY AND INDEX
page 24

WHAT IS A TERROR BIRD?

PHORUSRHACOS MEANS "RAG THIEF"

Phorusrhacos longissimus lived around 20 million to 4 million years ago, during the **Miocene and Pliocene periods**. **Fossils** of its skeleton have been found in South America and North America (see page 22).

It was flightless but could run at an average speed of 43 miles (69 km) per hour.

It had tiny wings with a hooked claw that may have gripped or slashed.

Its huge beak was hooked at the end, just like the beaks of modern birds of prey.

It used its beak like an ax to attack prey by pecking.

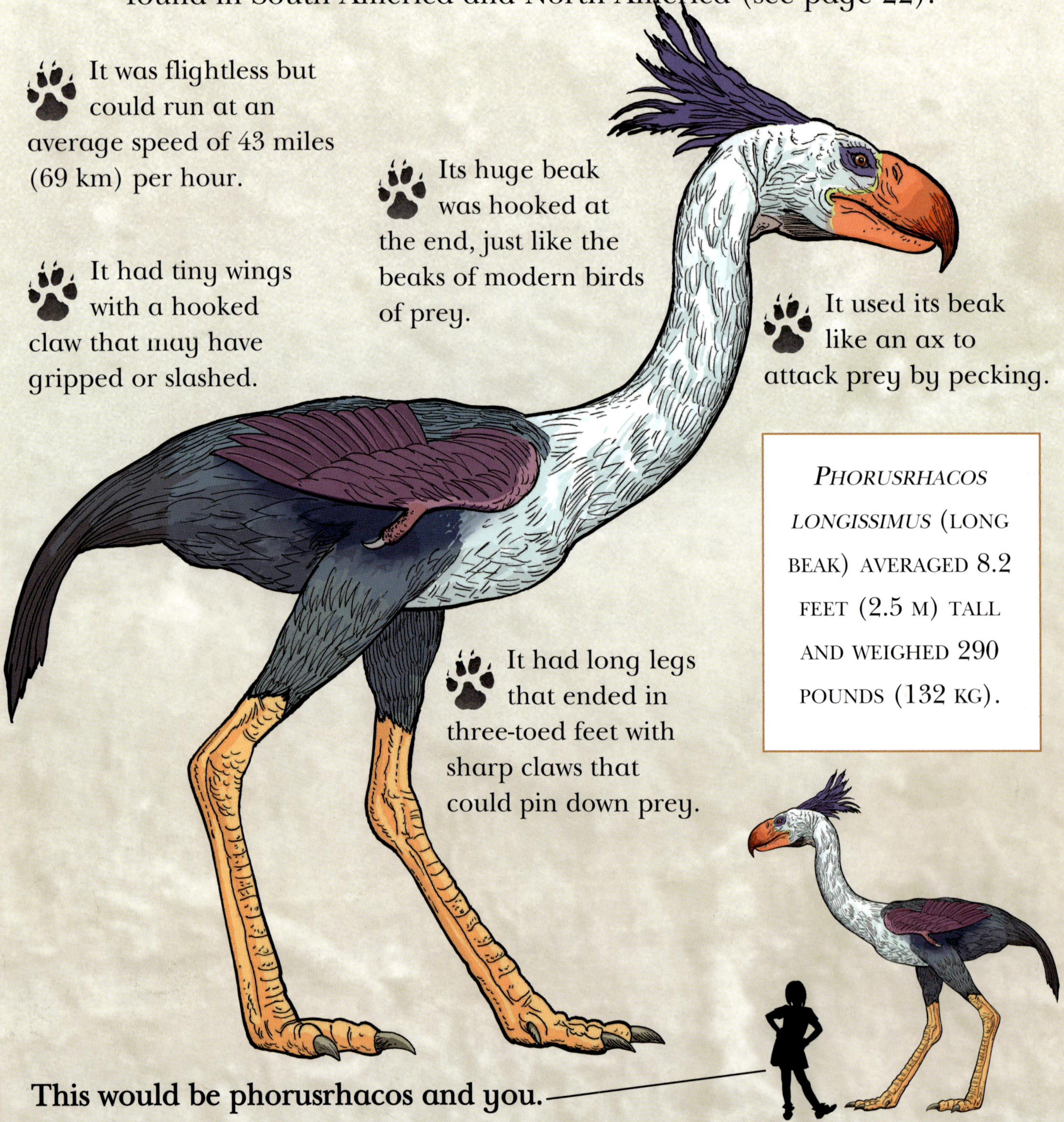

It had long legs that ended in three-toed feet with sharp claws that could pin down prey.

PHORUSRHACOS LONGISSIMUS (LONG BEAK) AVERAGED 8.2 FEET (2.5 M) TALL AND WEIGHED 290 POUNDS (132 KG).

This would be phorusrhacos and you.

TERROR BIRD FACTS

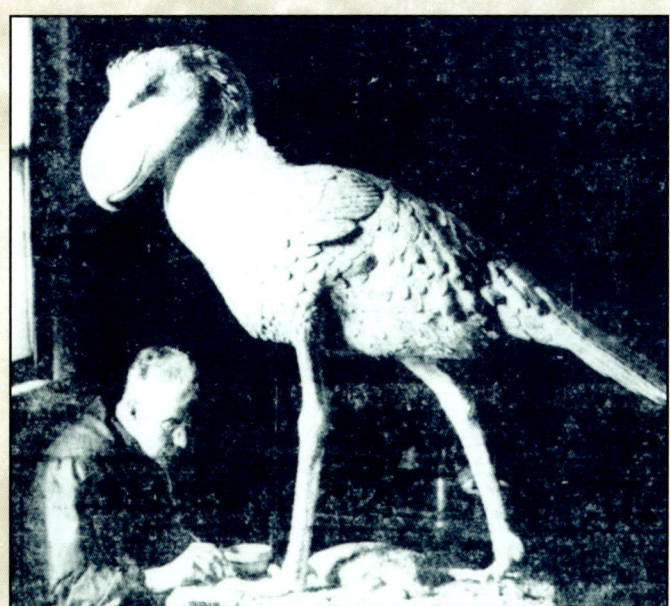

Terror birds evolved to be different sizes. Mesembriornis *was a fast-moving predator of the late Pliocene period.*

Terror birds first evolved in South America when it was separate from the rest of the world. The nearest competitors to terror birds were leopard-sized cats that haunted the forests. Terror birds' speed and fearsome beaks made them the top predators in South America for more than 50 million years. They lived in a landscape that slowly changed from jungle to grassy **savannah**. What they really looked like is unknown. Were they long-feathered like emus and rheas or short-feathered like eagles?

Phorusrhacos's neck was most powerful in a forward and backward pecking motion. It would not pick up prey and shake it. It would dig in its beak's hooked tip and use its strong neck muscles to rip back.

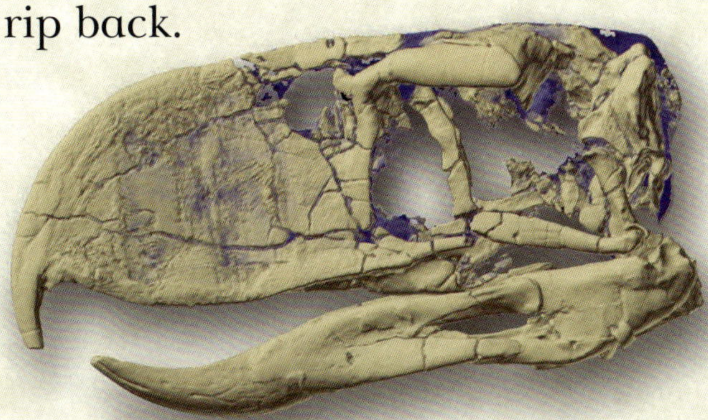

Today's large flightless birds have small heads and eat seeds, plants, and insects. The nearest modern bird to *phorusrhacos* is the seriema, a long-legged stalking bird that hunts lizards and snakes.

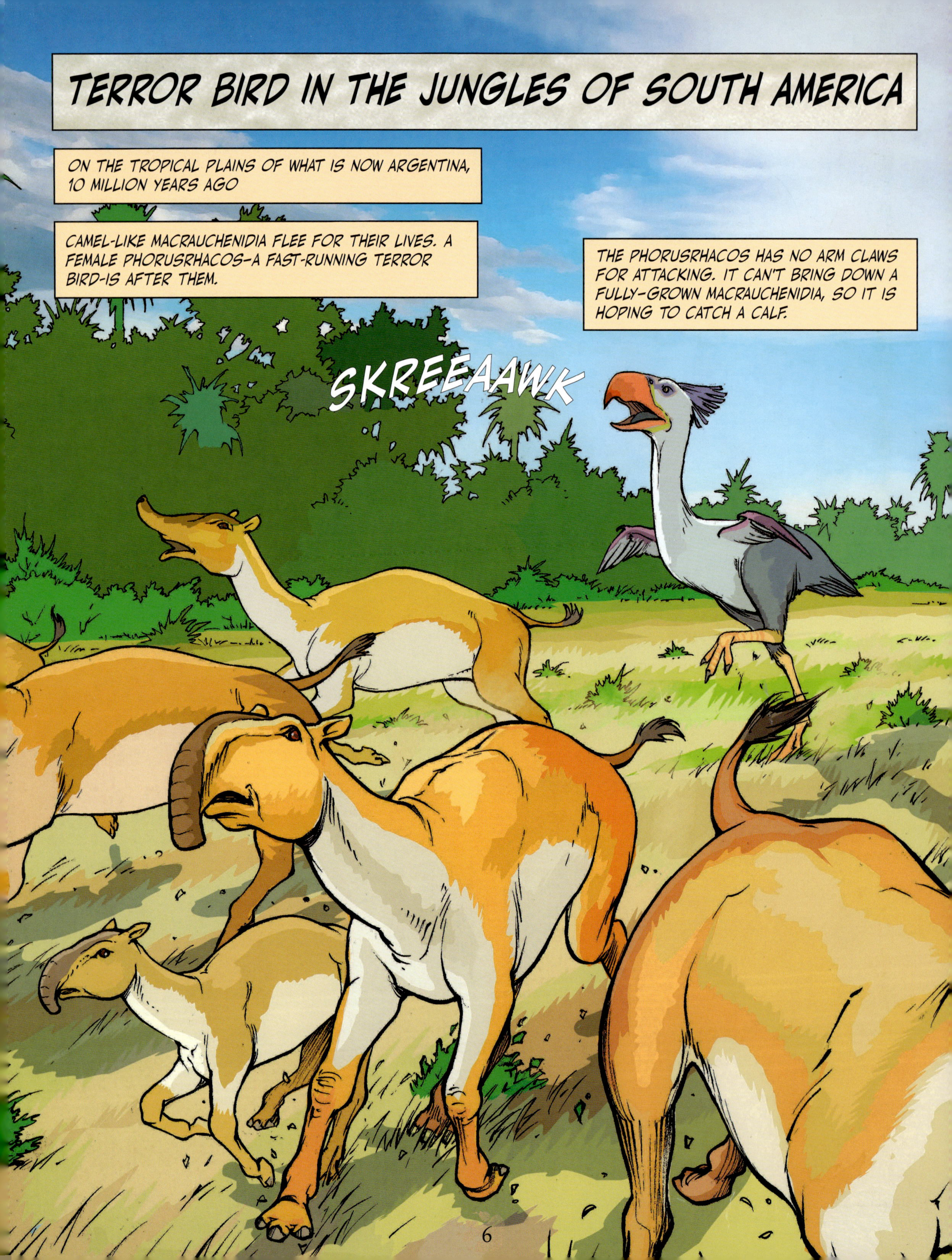
TERROR BIRD IN THE JUNGLES OF SOUTH AMERICA
ON THE TROPICAL PLAINS OF WHAT IS NOW ARGENTINA, 10 MILLION YEARS AGO
CAMEL-LIKE MACRAUCHENIDIA FLEE FOR THEIR LIVES. A FEMALE PHORUSRHACOS–A FAST-RUNNING TERROR BIRD–IS AFTER THEM.
THE PHORUSRHACOS HAS NO ARM CLAWS FOR ATTACKING. IT CAN'T BRING DOWN A FULLY-GROWN MACRAUCHENIDIA, SO IT IS HOPING TO CATCH A CALF.
SKREEAAWK

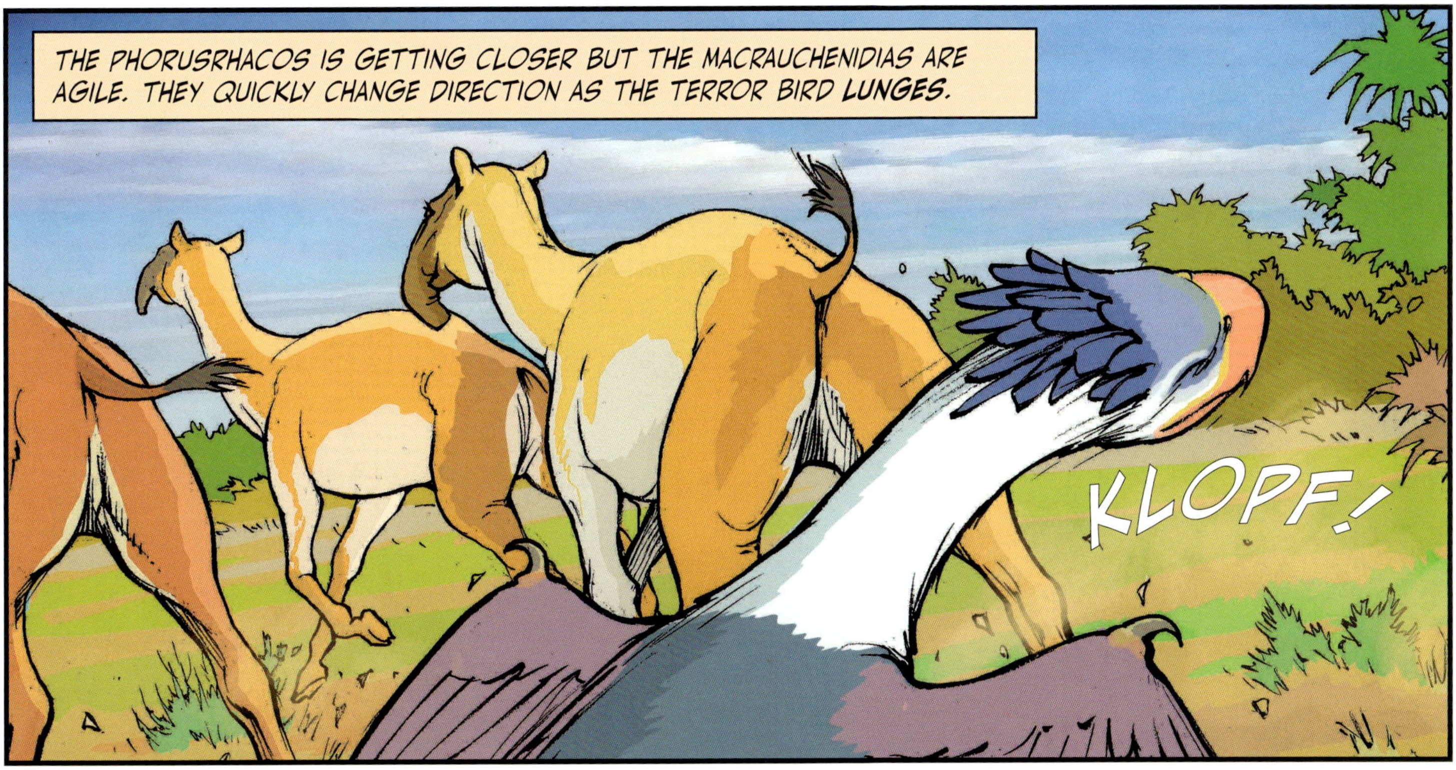
THE PHORUSRHACOS IS GETTING CLOSER BUT THE MACRAUCHENIDIAS ARE AGILE. THEY QUICKLY CHANGE DIRECTION AS THE TERROR BIRD **LUNGES**.
KLOPF!

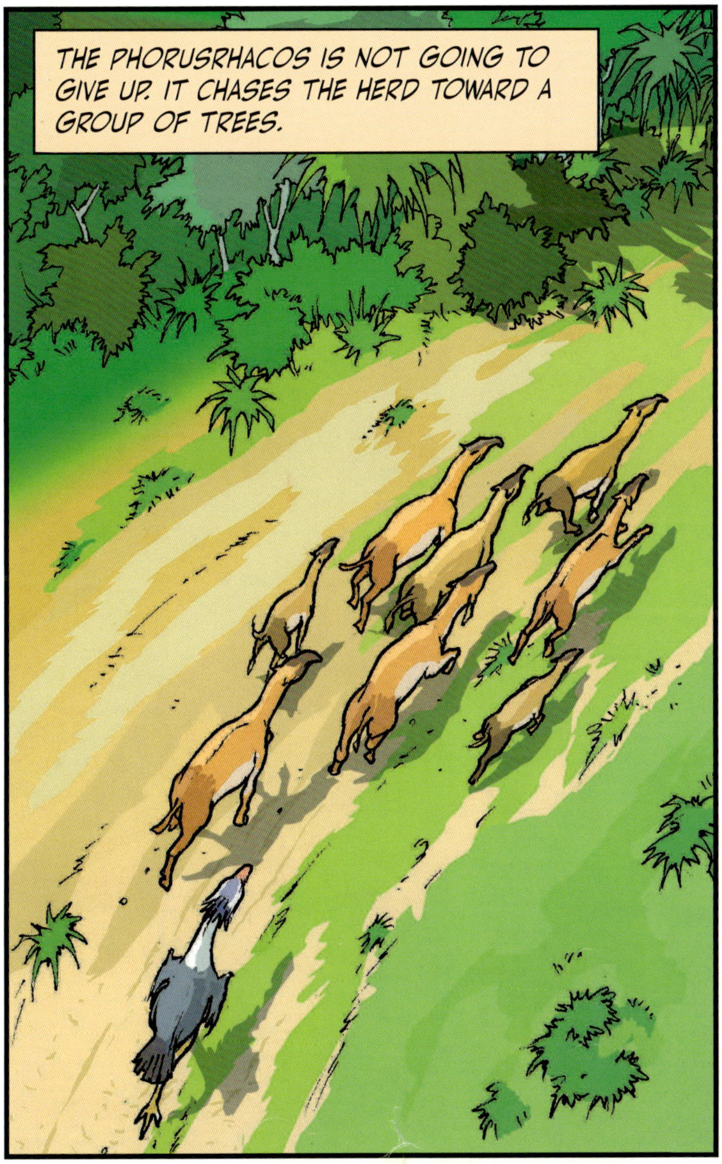
THE PHORUSRHACOS IS NOT GOING TO GIVE UP. IT CHASES THE HERD TOWARD A GROUP OF TREES.

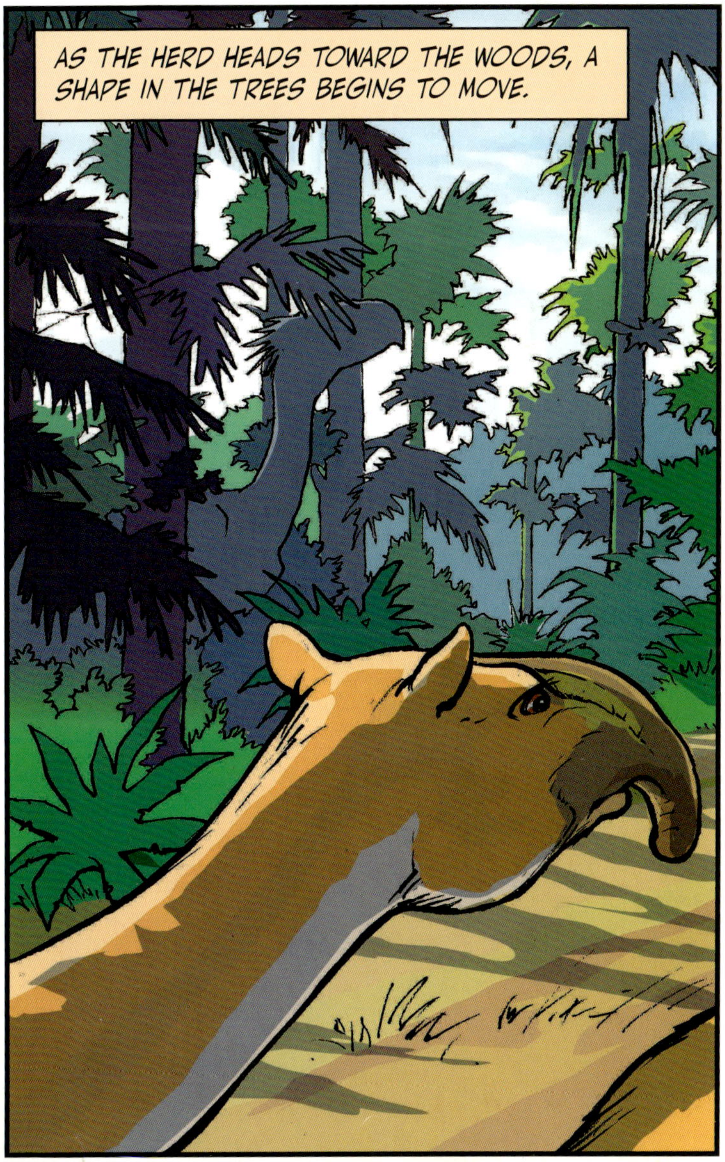
AS THE HERD HEADS TOWARD THE WOODS, A SHAPE IN THE TREES BEGINS TO MOVE.

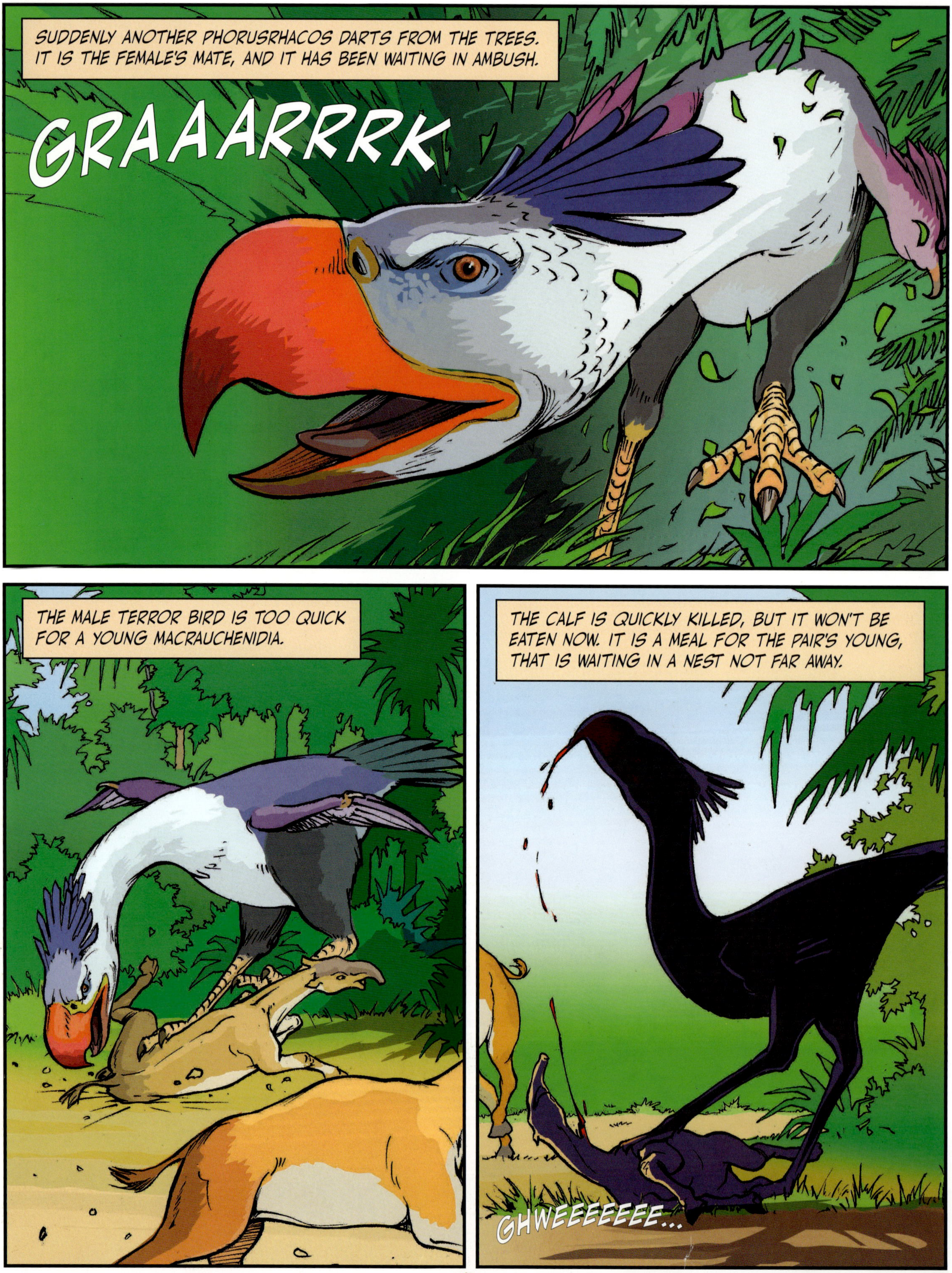
SUDDENLY ANOTHER PHORUSRHACOS DARTS FROM THE TREES. IT IS THE FEMALE'S MATE, AND IT HAS BEEN WAITING IN AMBUSH.
GRAAARRRK
THE MALE TERROR BIRD IS TOO QUICK FOR A YOUNG MACRAUCHENIDIA.
THE CALF IS QUICKLY KILLED, BUT IT WON'T BE EATEN NOW. IT IS A MEAL FOR THE PAIR'S YOUNG, THAT IS WAITING IN A NEST NOT FAR AWAY.
GHWEEEEEEE...

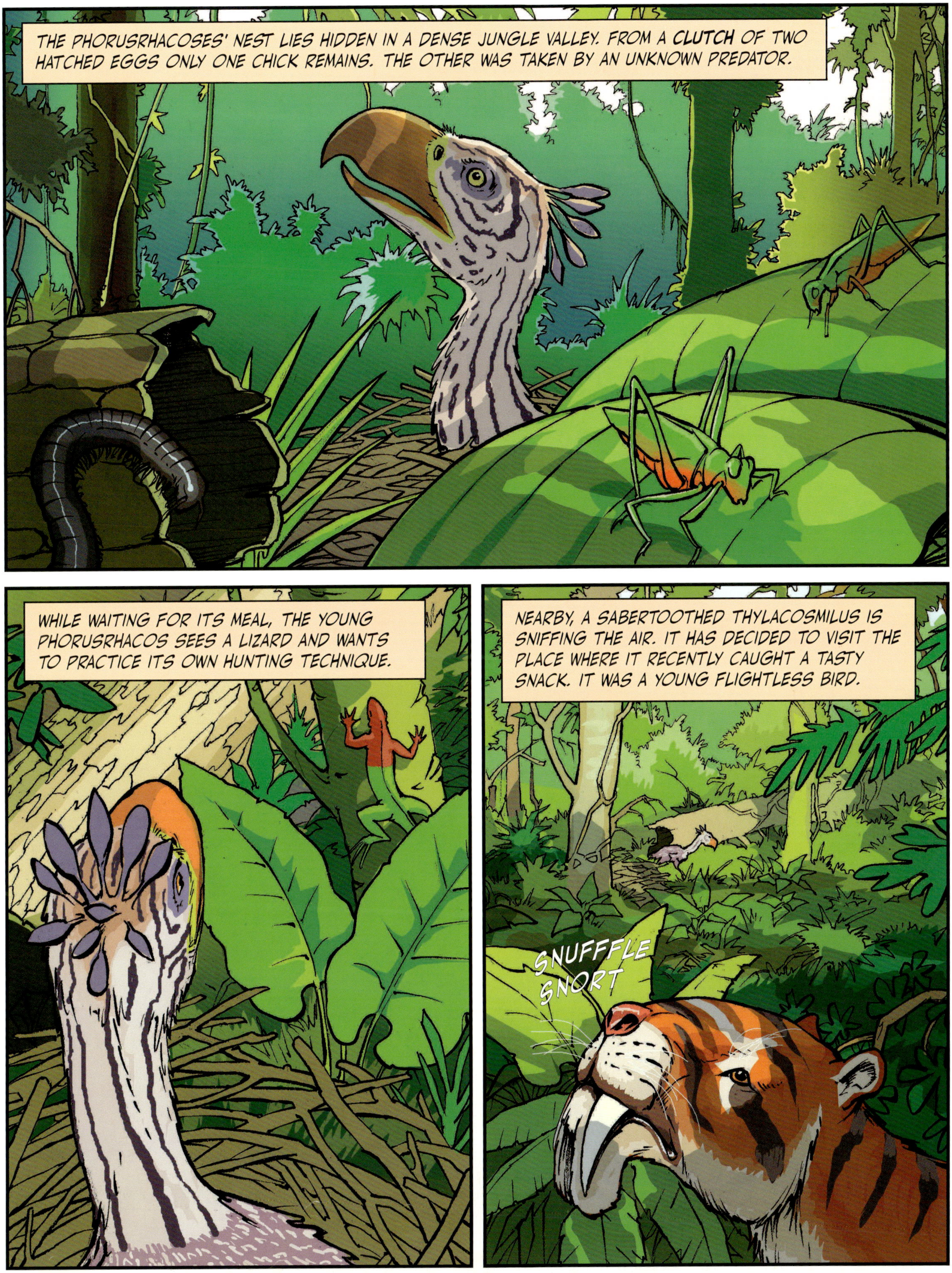
THE PHORUSRHACOSES' NEST LIES HIDDEN IN A DENSE JUNGLE VALLEY. FROM A CLUTCH OF TWO HATCHED EGGS ONLY ONE CHICK REMAINS. THE OTHER WAS TAKEN BY AN UNKNOWN PREDATOR.
WHILE WAITING FOR ITS MEAL, THE YOUNG PHORUSRHACOS SEES A LIZARD AND WANTS TO PRACTICE ITS OWN HUNTING TECHNIQUE.
NEARBY, A SABERTOOTHED THYLACOSMILUS IS SNIFFING THE AIR. IT HAS DECIDED TO VISIT THE PLACE WHERE IT RECENTLY CAUGHT A TASTY SNACK. IT WAS A YOUNG FLIGHTLESS BIRD.
SNUFFFLE
SNORT

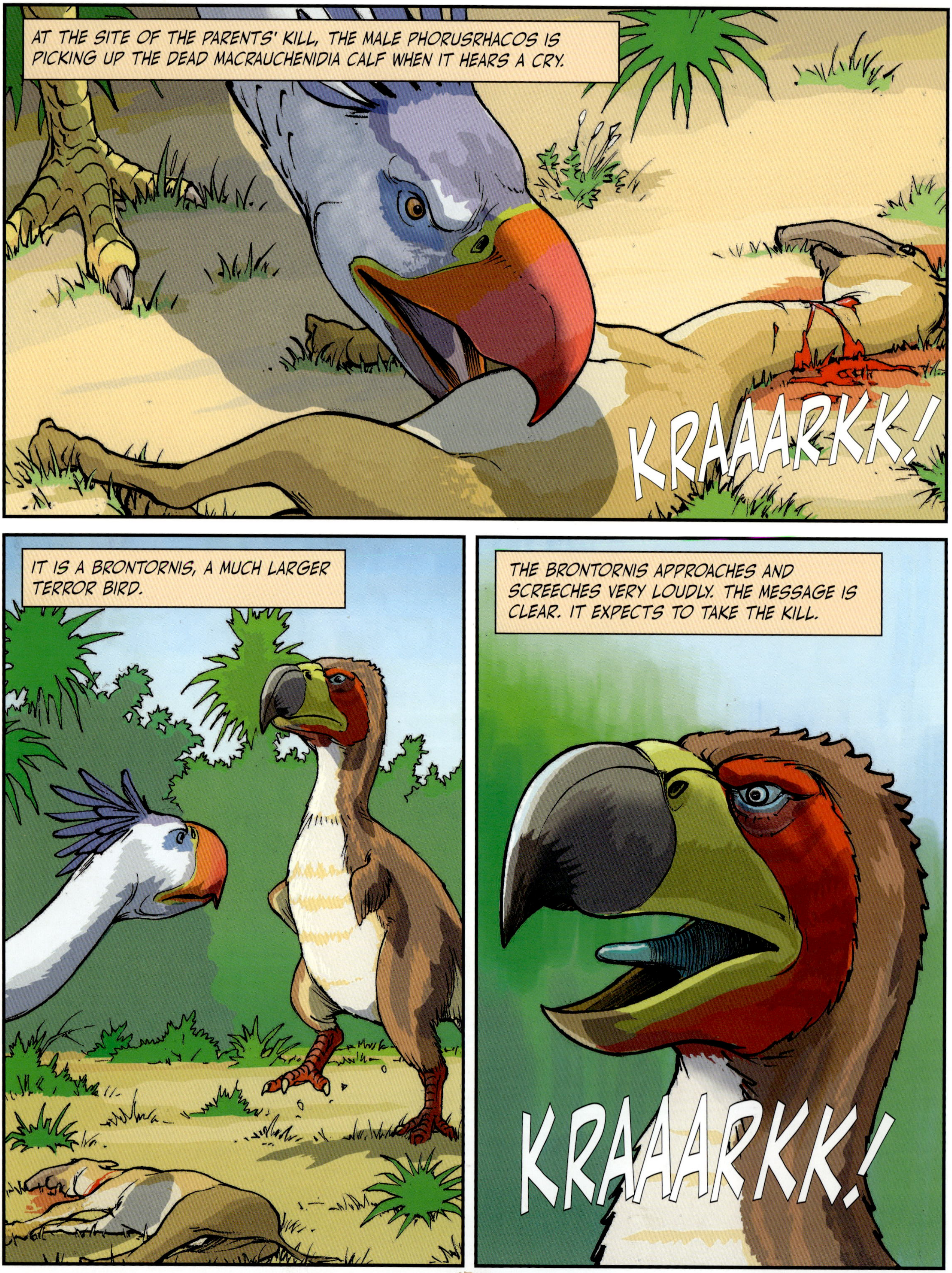
AT THE SITE OF THE PARENTS' KILL, THE MALE PHORUSRHACOS IS PICKING UP THE DEAD MACRAUCHENIDIA CALF WHEN IT HEARS A CRY.
KRAAARKK!
IT IS A BRONTORNIS, A MUCH LARGER TERROR BIRD.
THE BRONTORNIS APPROACHES AND SCREECHES VERY LOUDLY. THE MESSAGE IS CLEAR. IT EXPECTS TO TAKE THE KILL.
KRAAARKK!

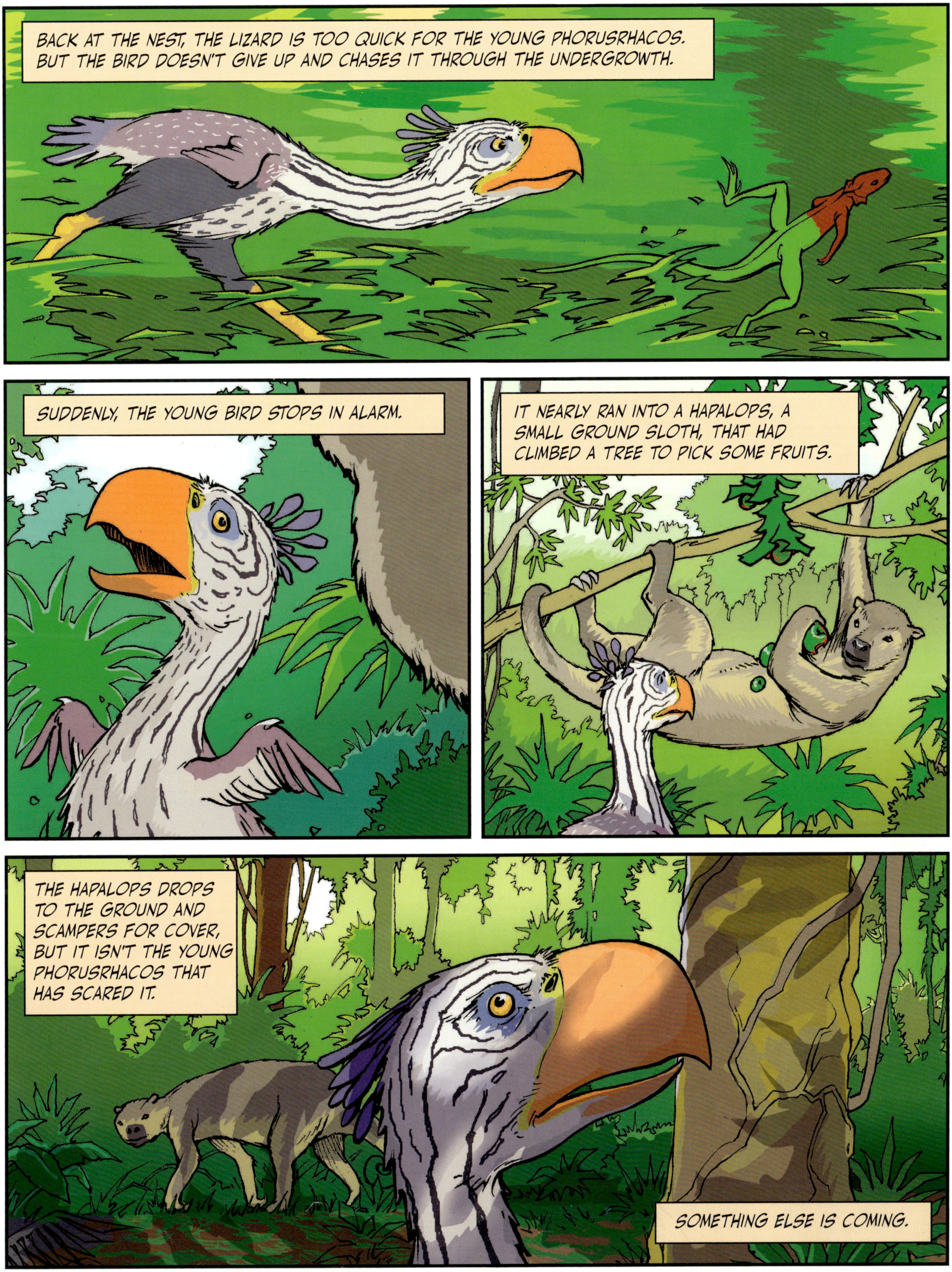
BACK AT THE NEST, THE LIZARD IS TOO QUICK FOR THE YOUNG PHORUSRHACOS. BUT THE BIRD DOESN'T GIVE UP AND CHASES IT THROUGH THE UNDERGROWTH.
SUDDENLY, THE YOUNG BIRD STOPS IN ALARM.
IT NEARLY RAN INTO A HAPALOPS, A SMALL GROUND SLOTH, THAT HAD CLIMBED A TREE TO PICK SOME FRUITS.
THE HAPALOPS DROPS TO THE GROUND AND SCAMPERS FOR COVER, BUT IT ISN'T THE YOUNG PHORUSRHACOS THAT HAS SCARED IT.
SOMETHING ELSE IS COMING.

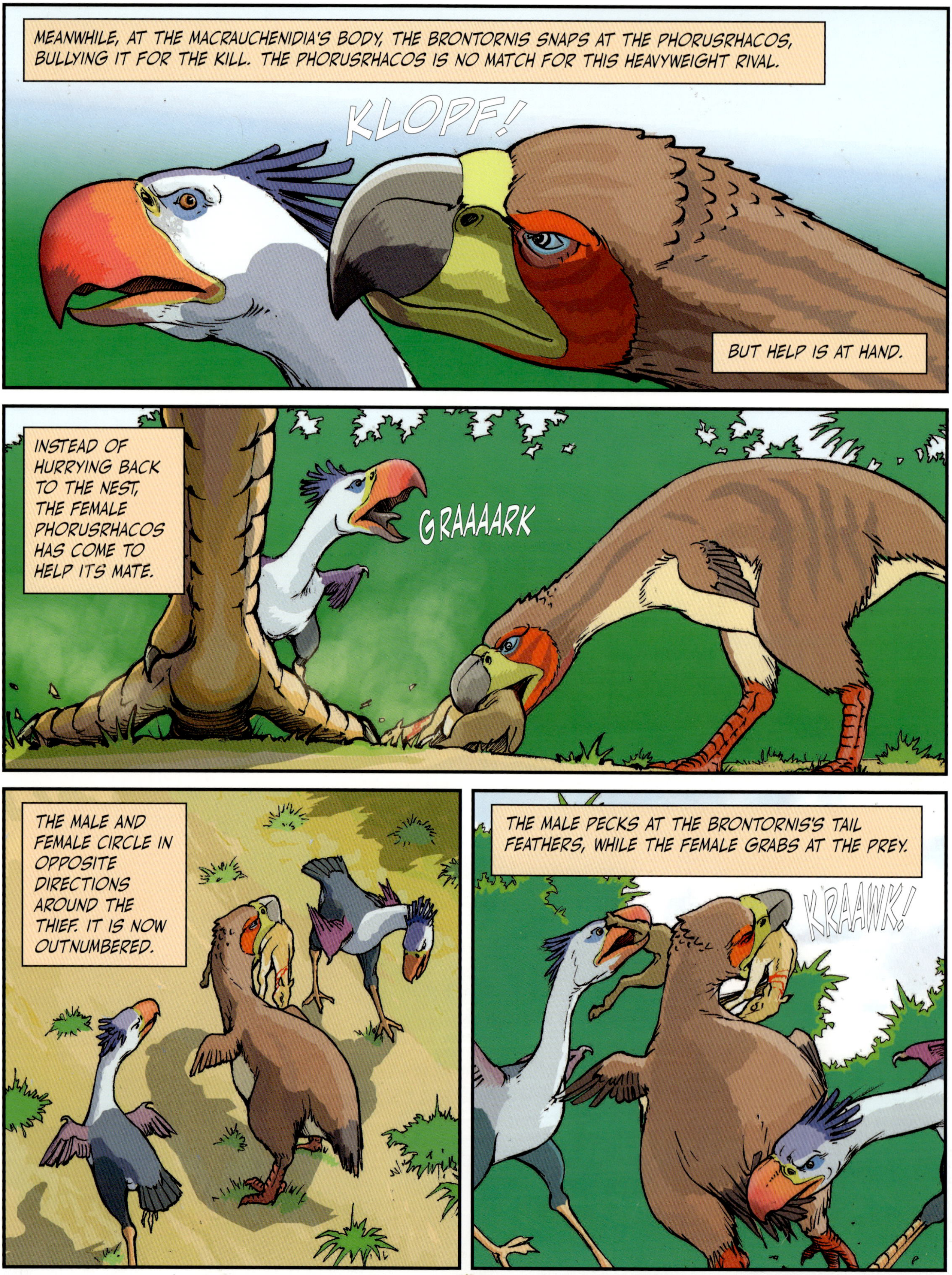
MEANWHILE, AT THE MACRAUCHENIDIA'S BODY, THE BRONTORNIS SNAPS AT THE PHORUSRHACOS, BULLYING IT FOR THE KILL. THE PHORUSRHACOS IS NO MATCH FOR THIS HEAVYWEIGHT RIVAL.
KLOPF!
BUT HELP IS AT HAND.
INSTEAD OF HURRYING BACK TO THE NEST, THE FEMALE PHORUSRHACOS HAS COME TO HELP ITS MATE.
GRAAAARK
THE MALE AND FEMALE CIRCLE IN OPPOSITE DIRECTIONS AROUND THE THIEF. IT IS NOW OUTNUMBERED.
THE MALE PECKS AT THE BRONTORNIS'S TAIL FEATHERS, WHILE THE FEMALE GRABS AT THE PREY.
KRAAWK!

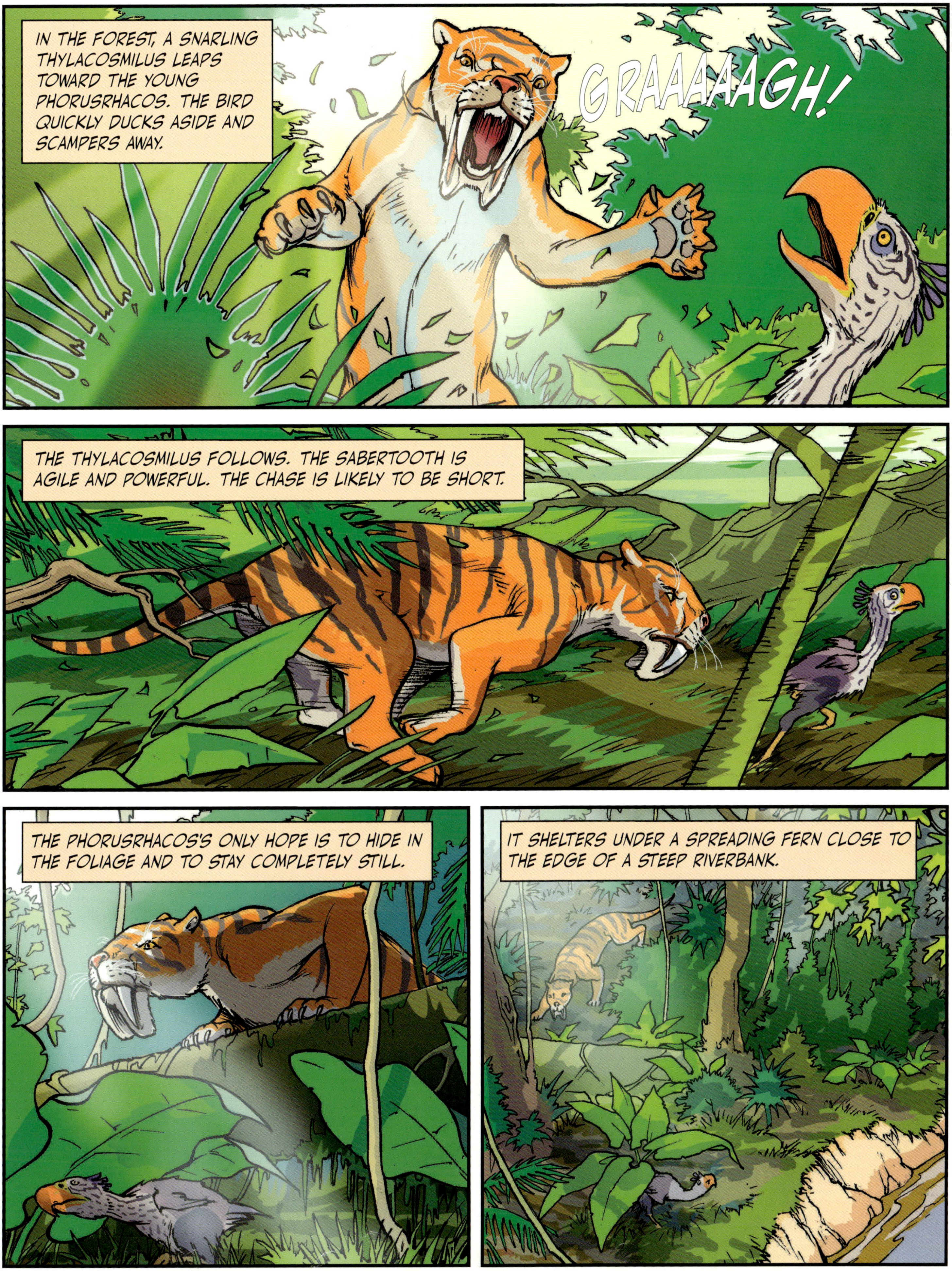
IN THE FOREST, A SNARLING THYLACOSMILUS LEAPS TOWARD THE YOUNG PHORUSRHACOS. THE BIRD QUICKLY DUCKS ASIDE AND SCAMPERS AWAY.
GRAAAAAGH!
THE THYLACOSMILUS FOLLOWS. THE SABERTOOTH IS AGILE AND POWERFUL. THE CHASE IS LIKELY TO BE SHORT.
THE PHORUSRHACOS'S ONLY HOPE IS TO HIDE IN THE FOLIAGE AND TO STAY COMPLETELY STILL.
IT SHELTERS UNDER A SPREADING FERN CLOSE TO THE EDGE OF A STEEP RIVERBANK.

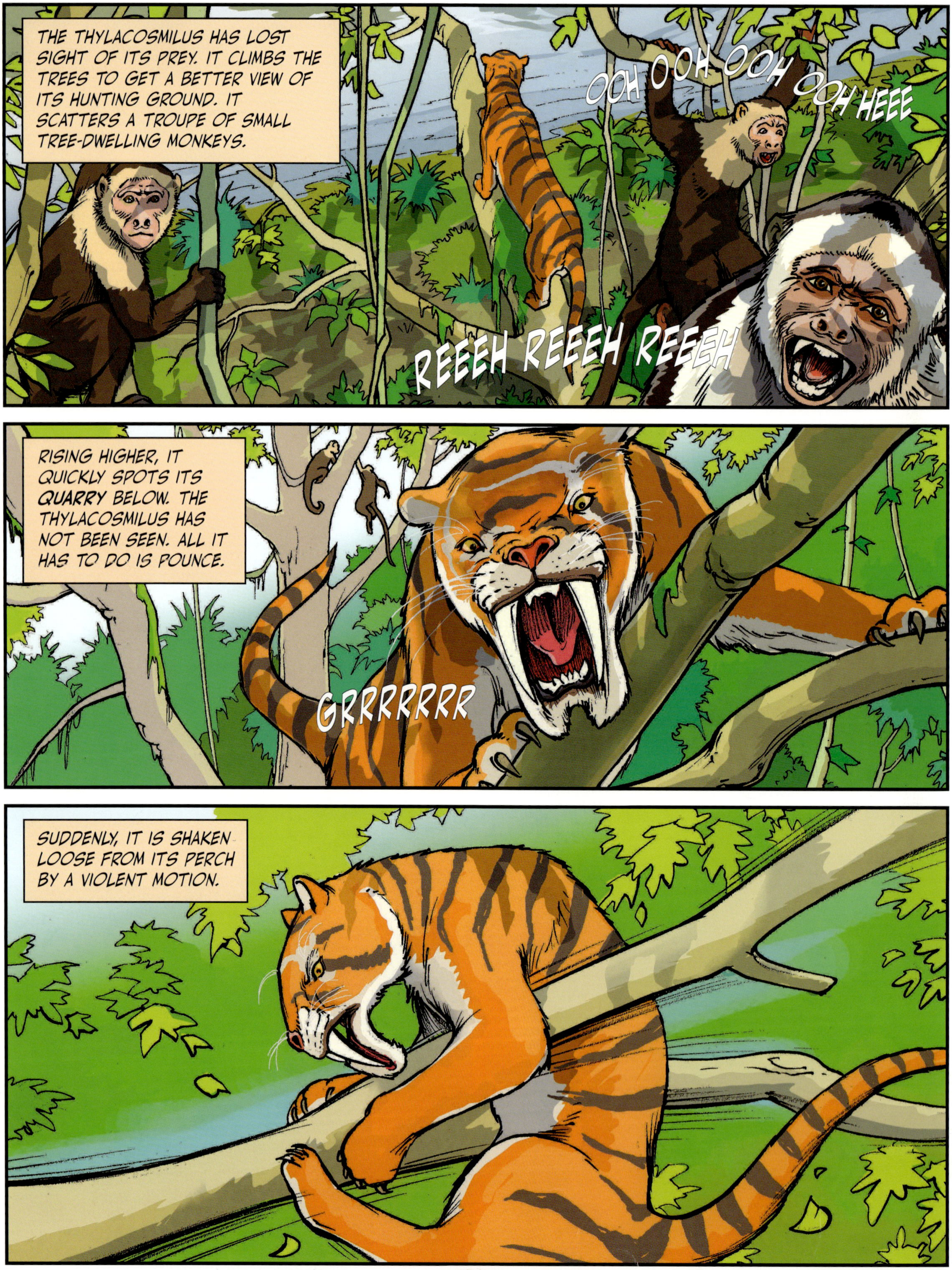
THE THYLACOSMILUS HAS LOST SIGHT OF ITS PREY. IT CLIMBS THE TREES TO GET A BETTER VIEW OF ITS HUNTING GROUND. IT SCATTERS A TROUPE OF SMALL TREE-DWELLING MONKEYS.
OOH OOH OOH OOH HEEE
REEEH REEEH REEEH
RISING HIGHER, IT QUICKLY SPOTS ITS **QUARRY** BELOW. THE THYLACOSMILUS HAS NOT BEEN SEEN. ALL IT HAS TO DO IS POUNCE.
GRRRRRRR
SUDDENLY, IT IS SHAKEN LOOSE FROM ITS PERCH BY A VIOLENT MOTION.

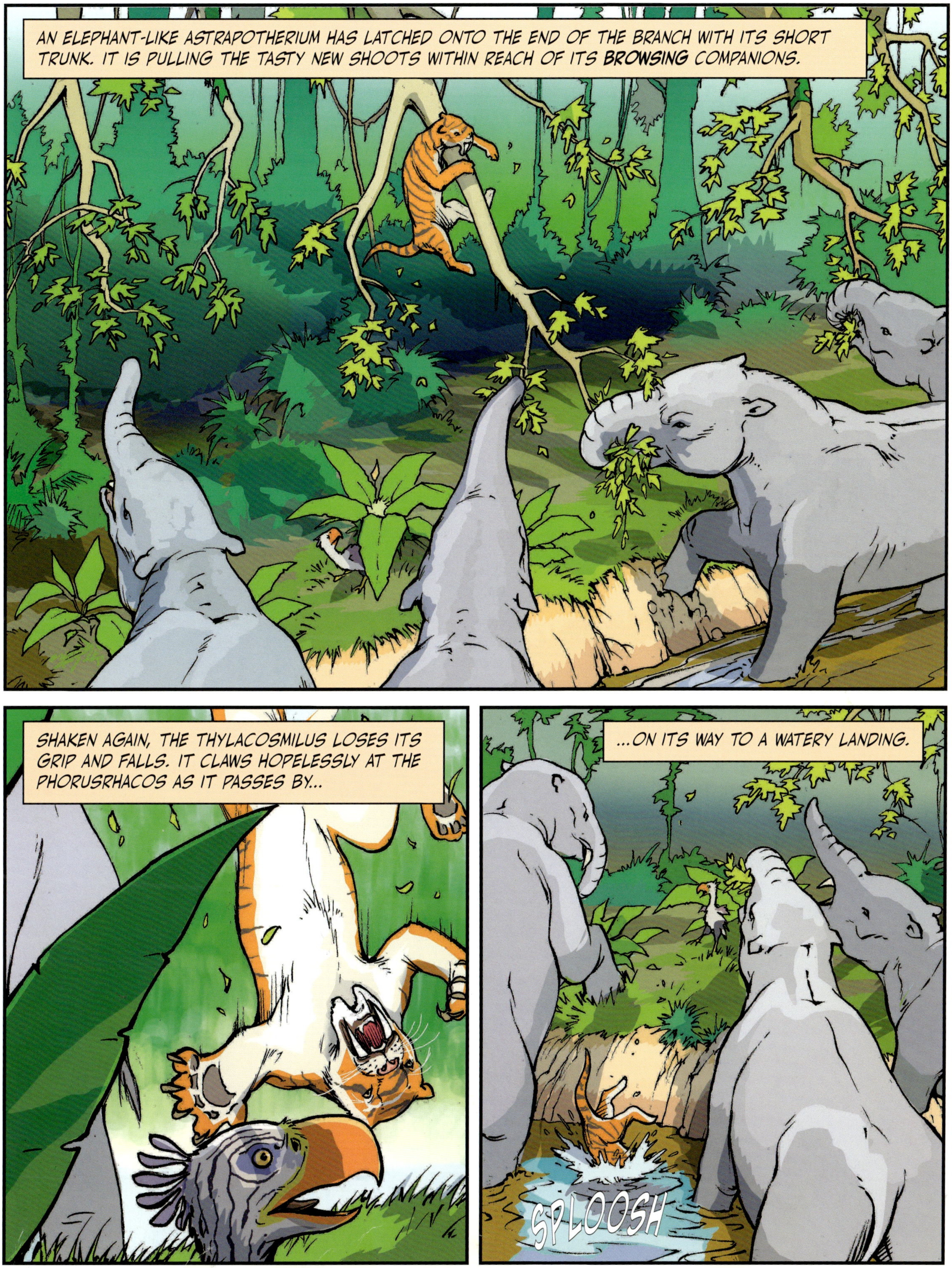
AN ELEPHANT-LIKE ASTRAPOTHERIUM HAS LATCHED ONTO THE END OF THE BRANCH WITH ITS SHORT TRUNK. IT IS PULLING THE TASTY NEW SHOOTS WITHIN REACH OF ITS **BROWSING** COMPANIONS.
SHAKEN AGAIN, THE THYLACOSMILUS LOSES ITS GRIP AND FALLS. IT CLAWS HOPELESSLY AT THE PHORUSRHACOS AS IT PASSES BY...
...ON ITS WAY TO A WATERY LANDING.
SPLOOSH

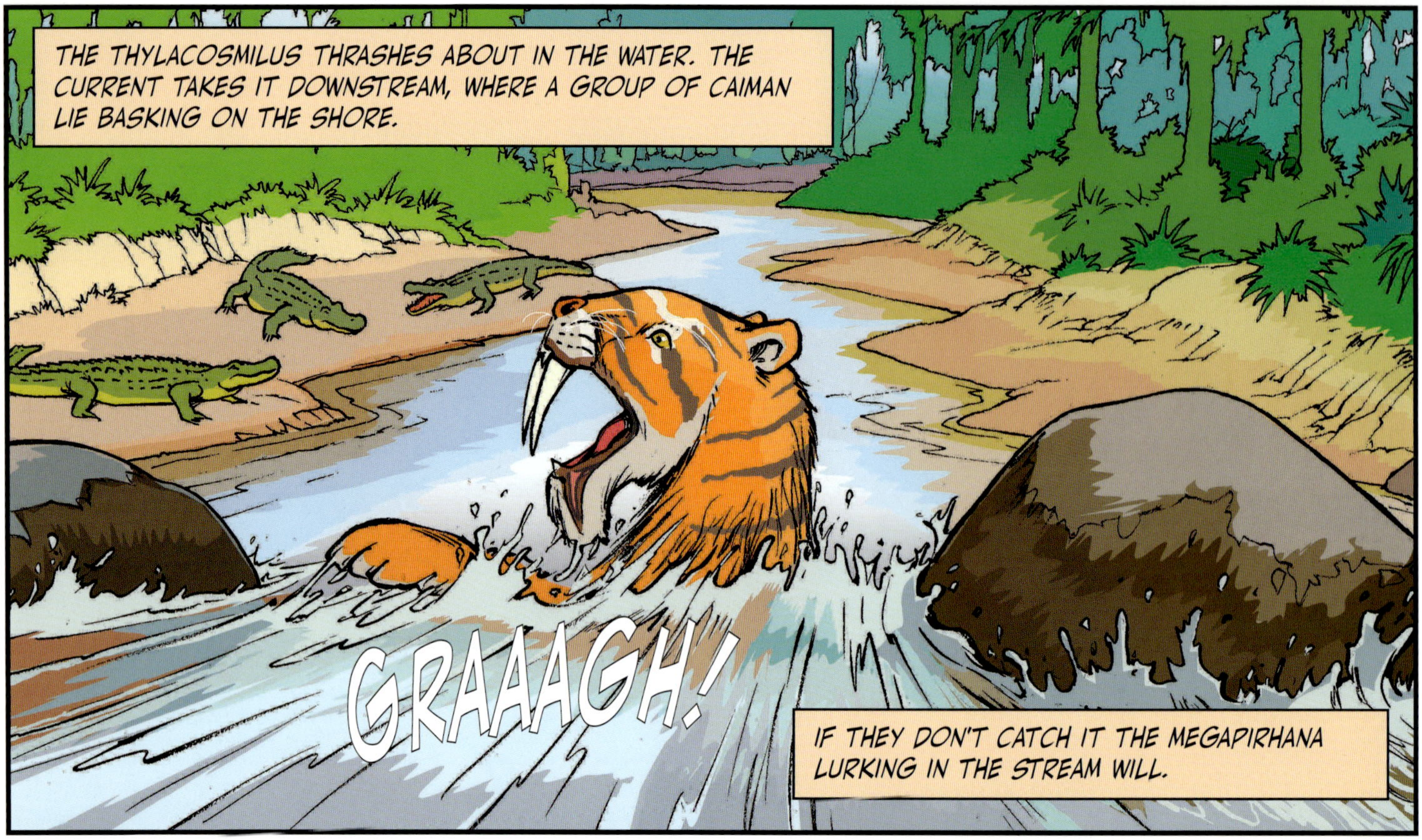
THE THYLACOSMILUS THRASHES ABOUT IN THE WATER. THE CURRENT TAKES IT DOWNSTREAM, WHERE A GROUP OF CAIMAN LIE BASKING ON THE SHORE.
GRAAAGH!
IF THEY DON'T CATCH IT THE MEGAPIRHANA LURKING IN THE STREAM WILL.

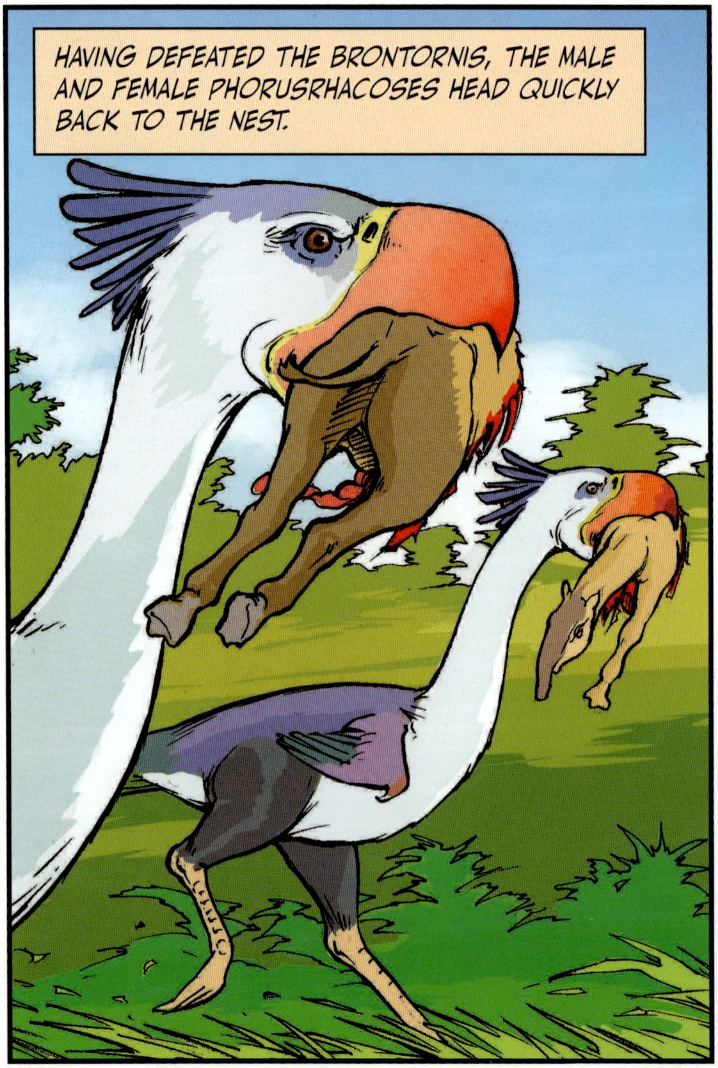
HAVING DEFEATED THE BRONTORNIS, THE MALE AND FEMALE PHORUSRHACOSES HEAD QUICKLY BACK TO THE NEST.

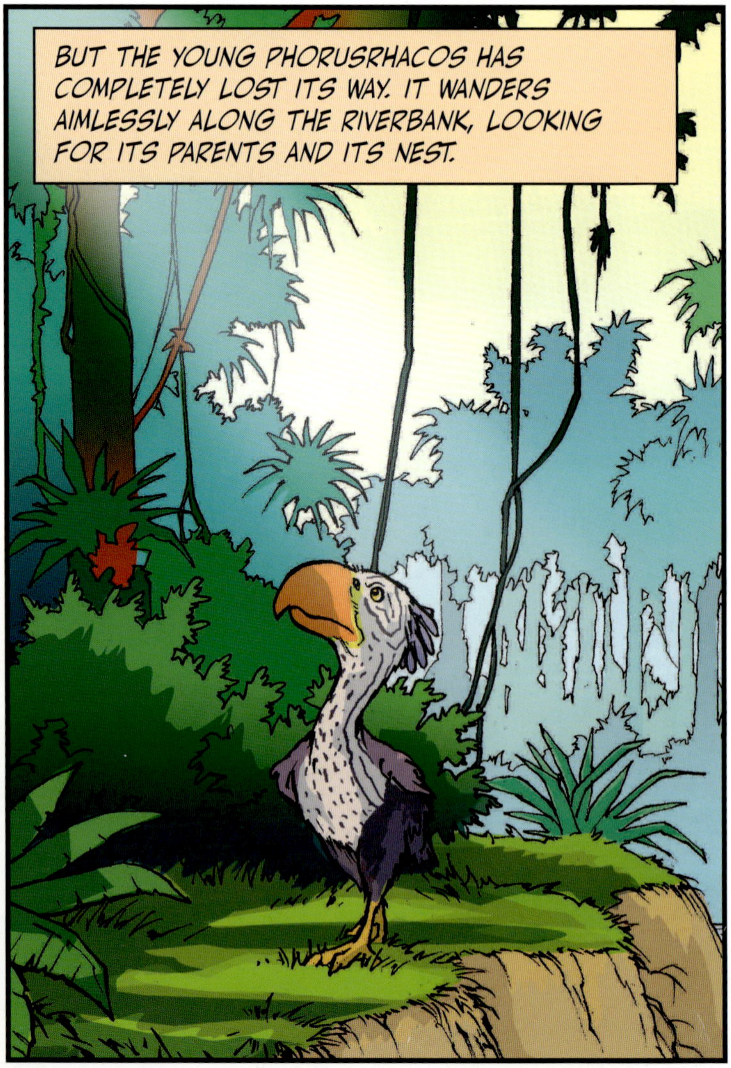
BUT THE YOUNG PHORUSRHACOS HAS COMPLETELY LOST ITS WAY. IT WANDERS AIMLESSLY ALONG THE RIVERBANK, LOOKING FOR ITS PARENTS AND ITS NEST.

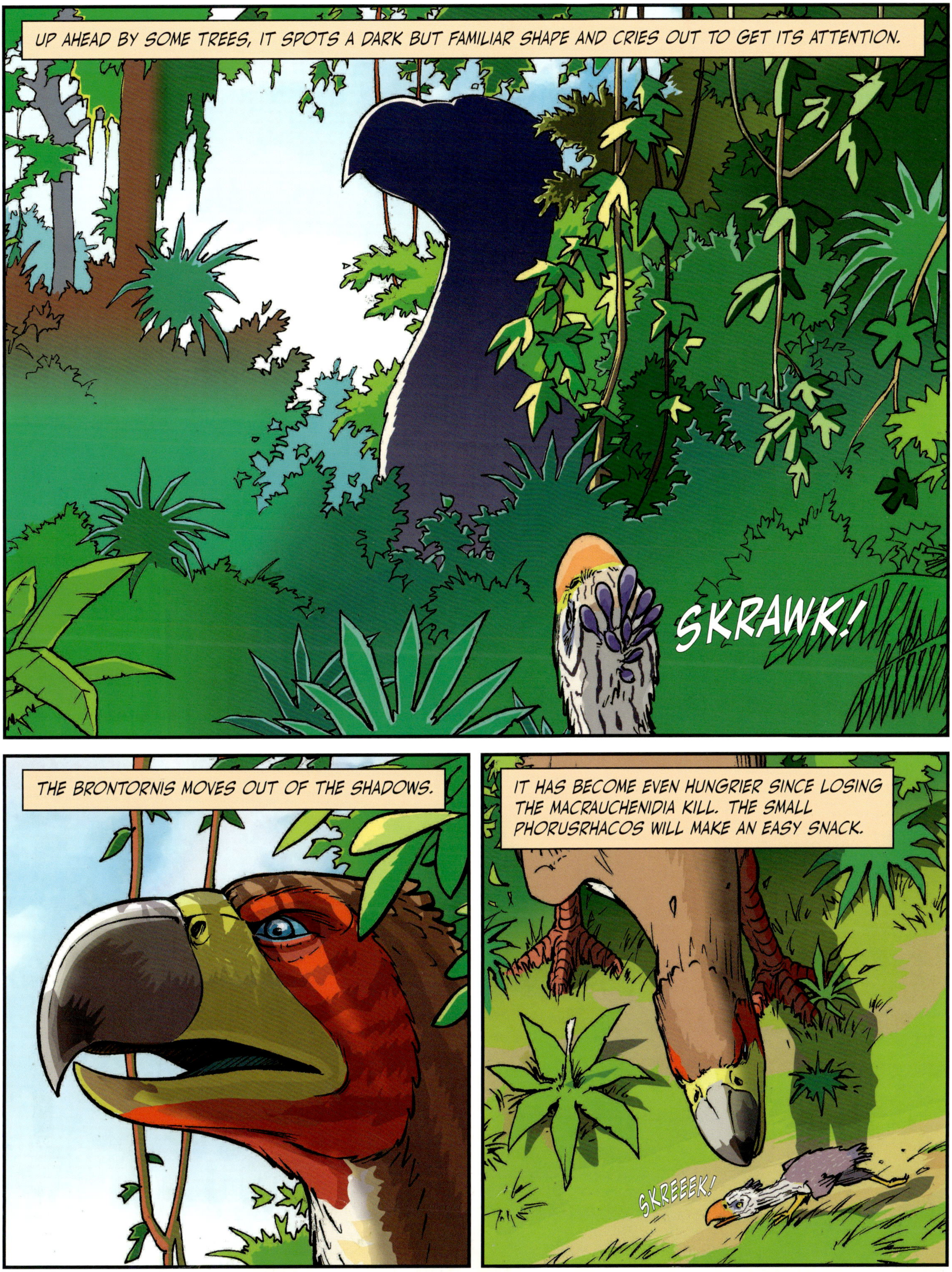
UP AHEAD BY SOME TREES, IT SPOTS A DARK BUT FAMILIAR SHAPE AND CRIES OUT TO GET ITS ATTENTION.
SKRAWK!
THE BRONTORNIS MOVES OUT OF THE SHADOWS.
IT HAS BECOME EVEN HUNGRIER SINCE LOSING THE MACRAUCHENIDIA KILL. THE SMALL PHORUSRHACOS WILL MAKE AN EASY SNACK.
SKREEEK!

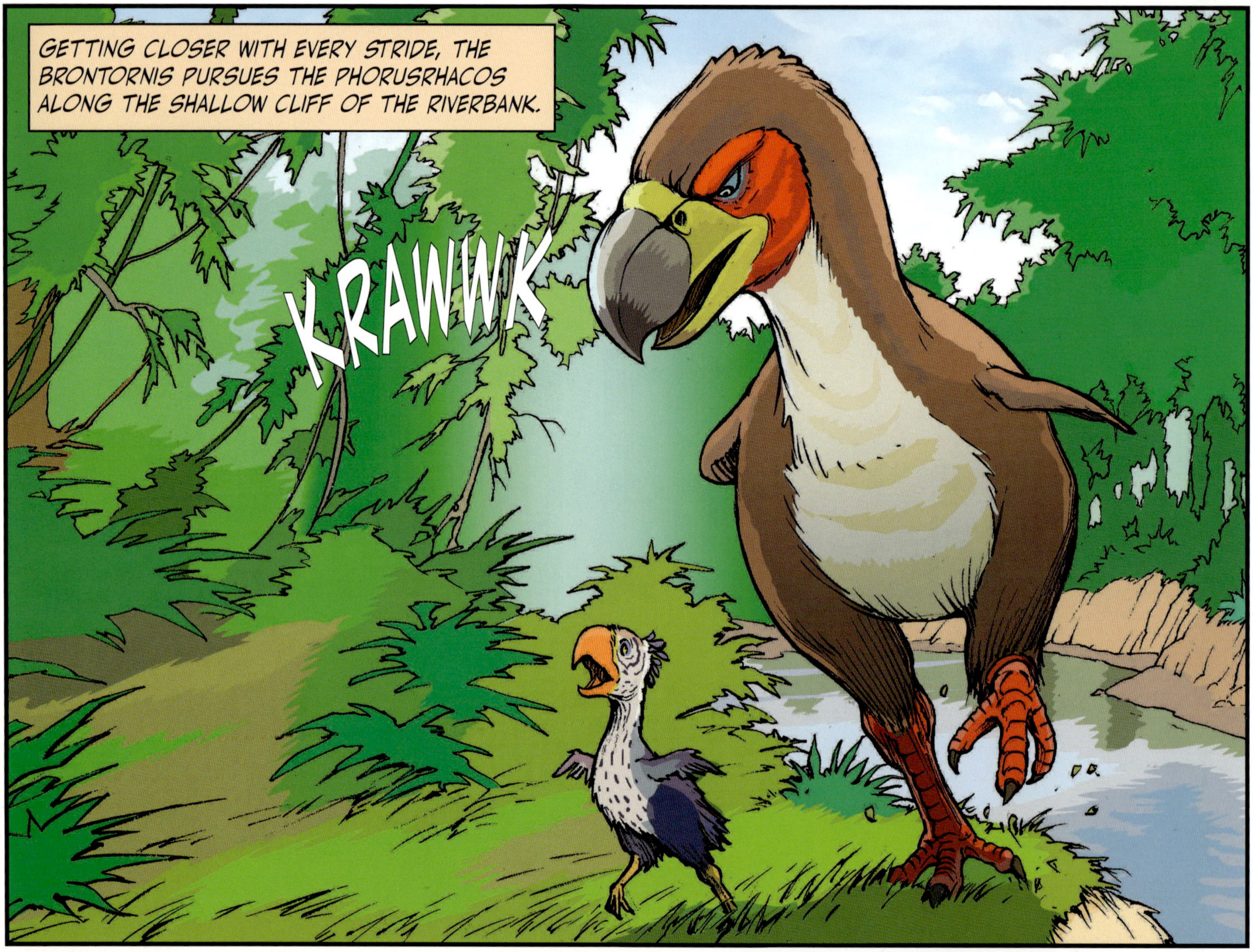
GETTING CLOSER WITH EVERY STRIDE, THE BRONTORNIS PURSUES THE PHORUSRHACOS ALONG THE SHALLOW CLIFF OF THE RIVERBANK.
KRAWWK

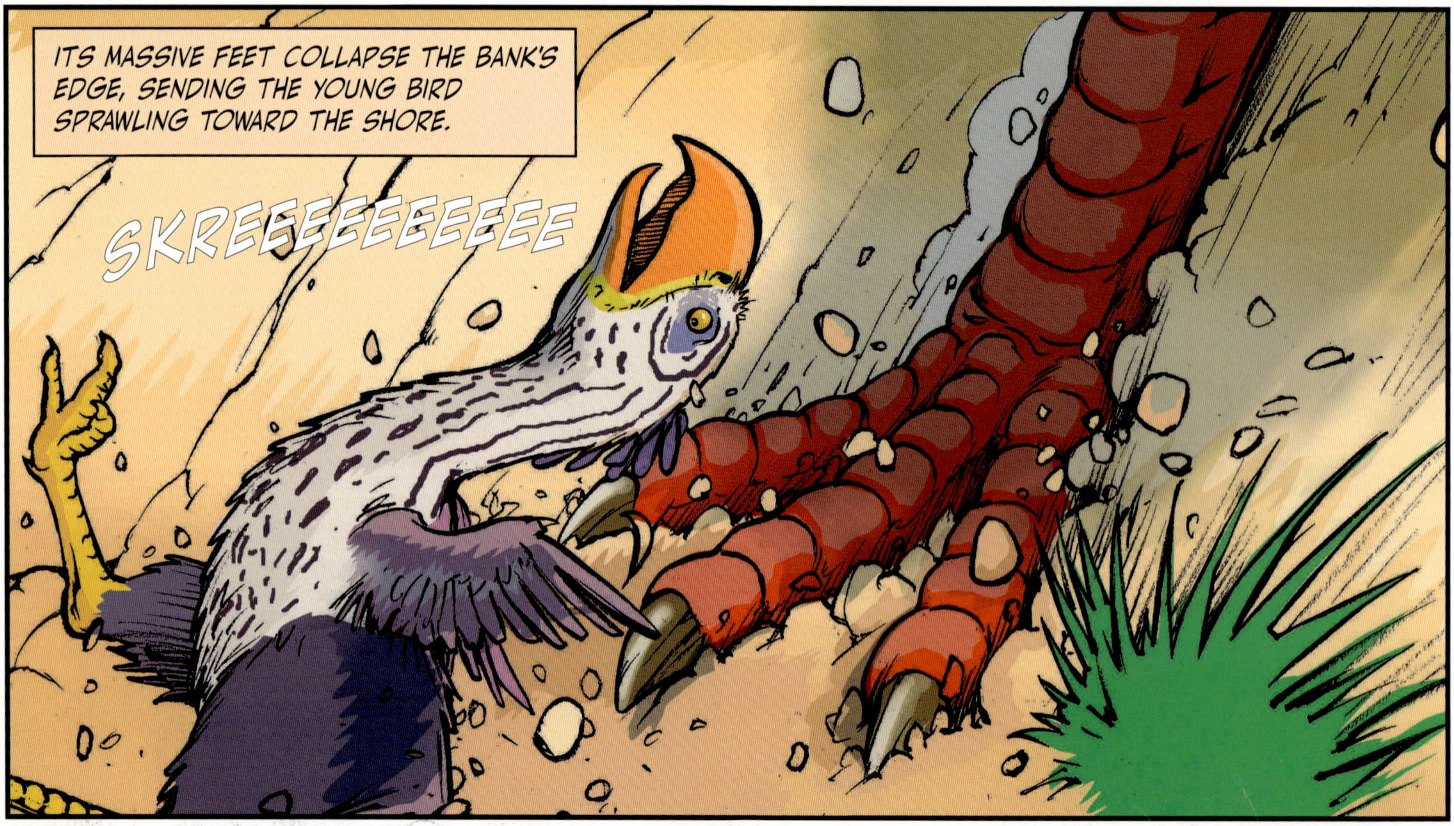
ITS MASSIVE FEET COLLAPSE THE BANK'S EDGE, SENDING THE YOUNG BIRD SPRAWLING TOWARD THE SHORE.
SKREEEEEEEEEEE

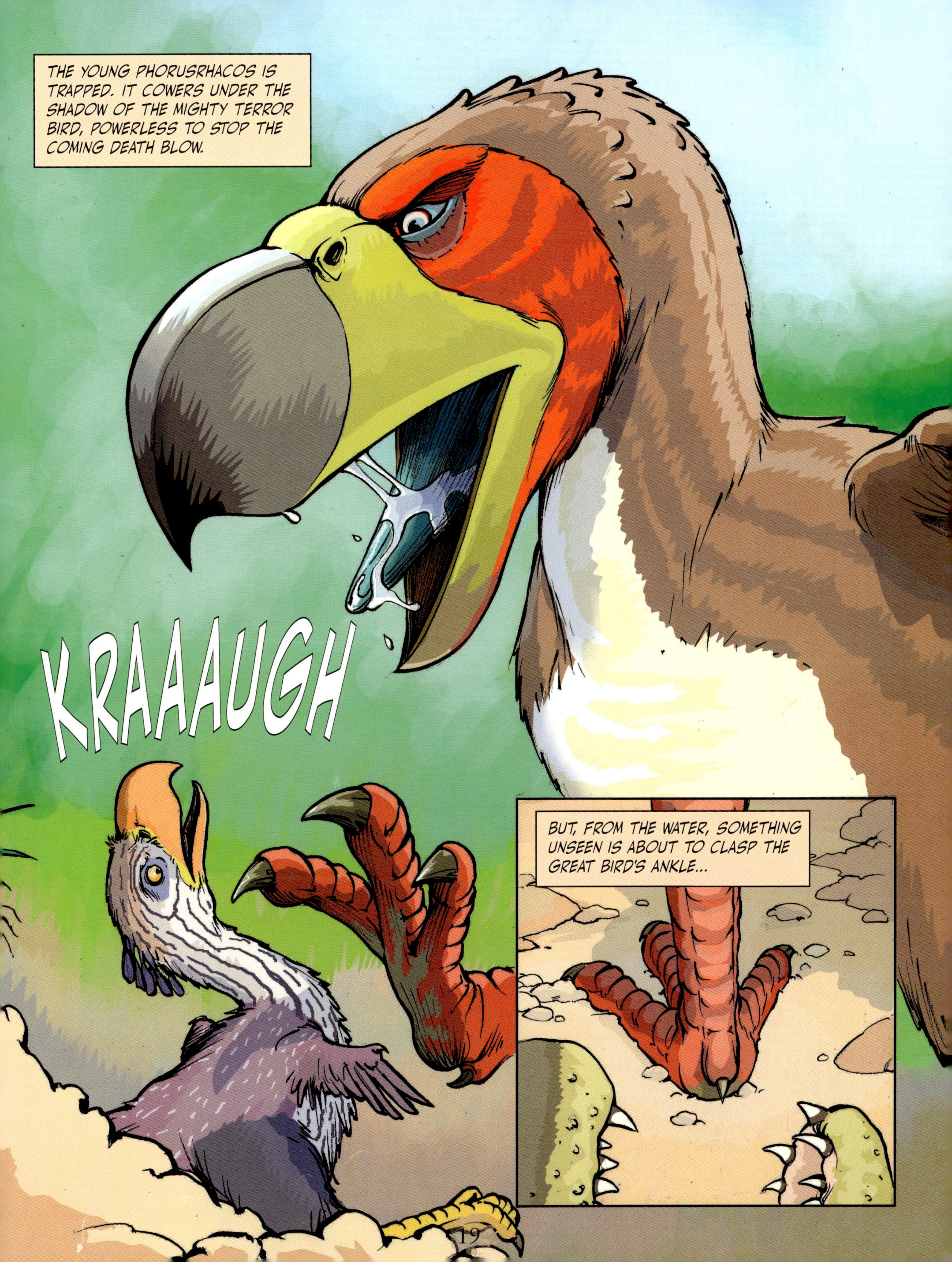
THE YOUNG PHORUSRHACOS IS TRAPPED. IT COWERS UNDER THE SHADOW OF THE MIGHTY TERROR BIRD, POWERLESS TO STOP THE COMING DEATH BLOW.
KRAAAUGH
BUT, FROM THE WATER, SOMETHING UNSEEN IS ABOUT TO CLASP THE GREAT BIRD'S ANKLE...

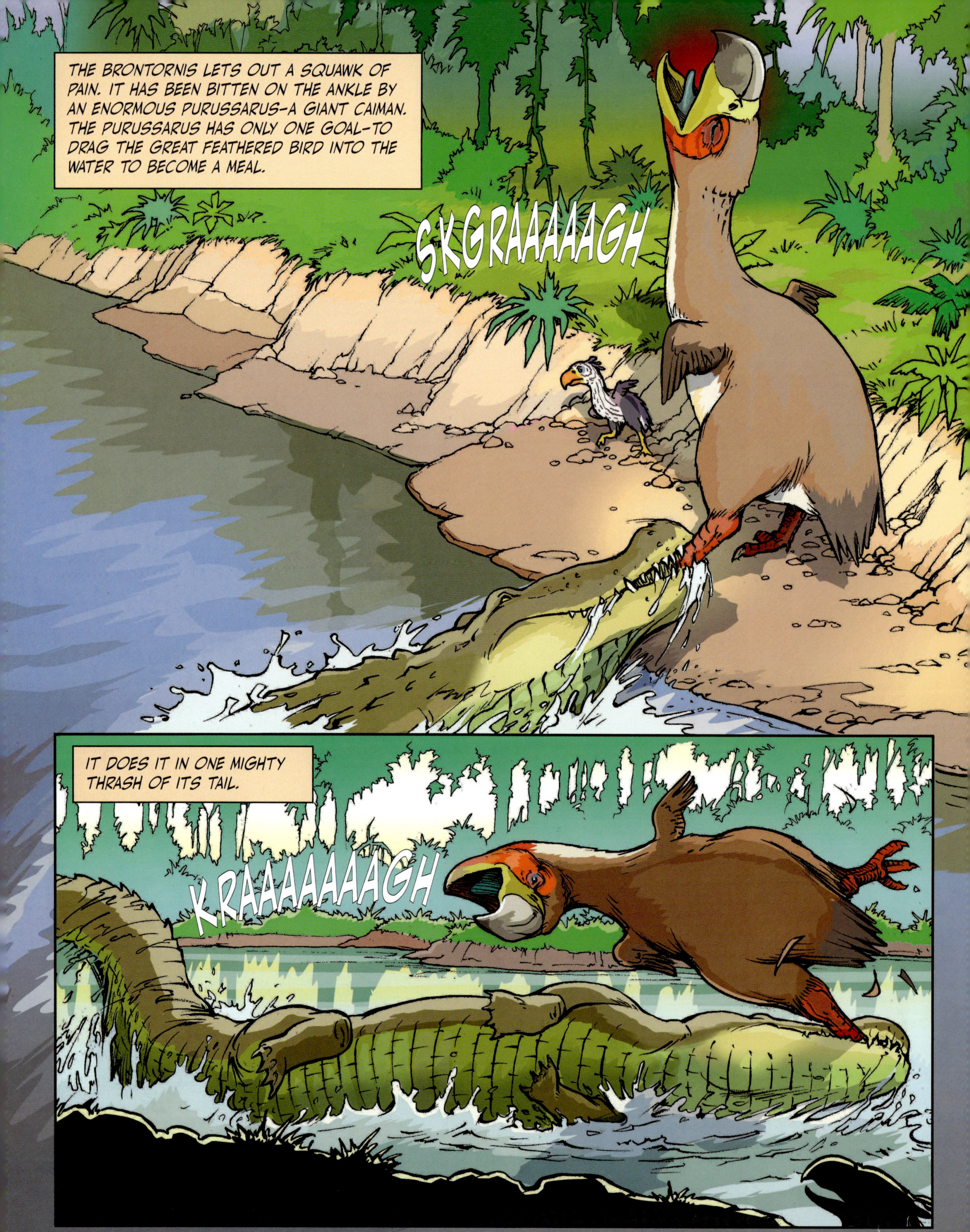
THE BRONTORNIS LETS OUT A SQUAWK OF PAIN. IT HAS BEEN BITTEN ON THE ANKLE BY AN ENORMOUS PURUSSARUS–A GIANT CAIMAN. THE PURUSSARUS HAS ONLY ONE GOAL–TO DRAG THE GREAT FEATHERED BIRD INTO THE WATER TO BECOME A MEAL.
SKGRAAAAAGH
IT DOES IT IN ONE MIGHTY THRASH OF ITS TAIL.
KRAAAAAAAGH

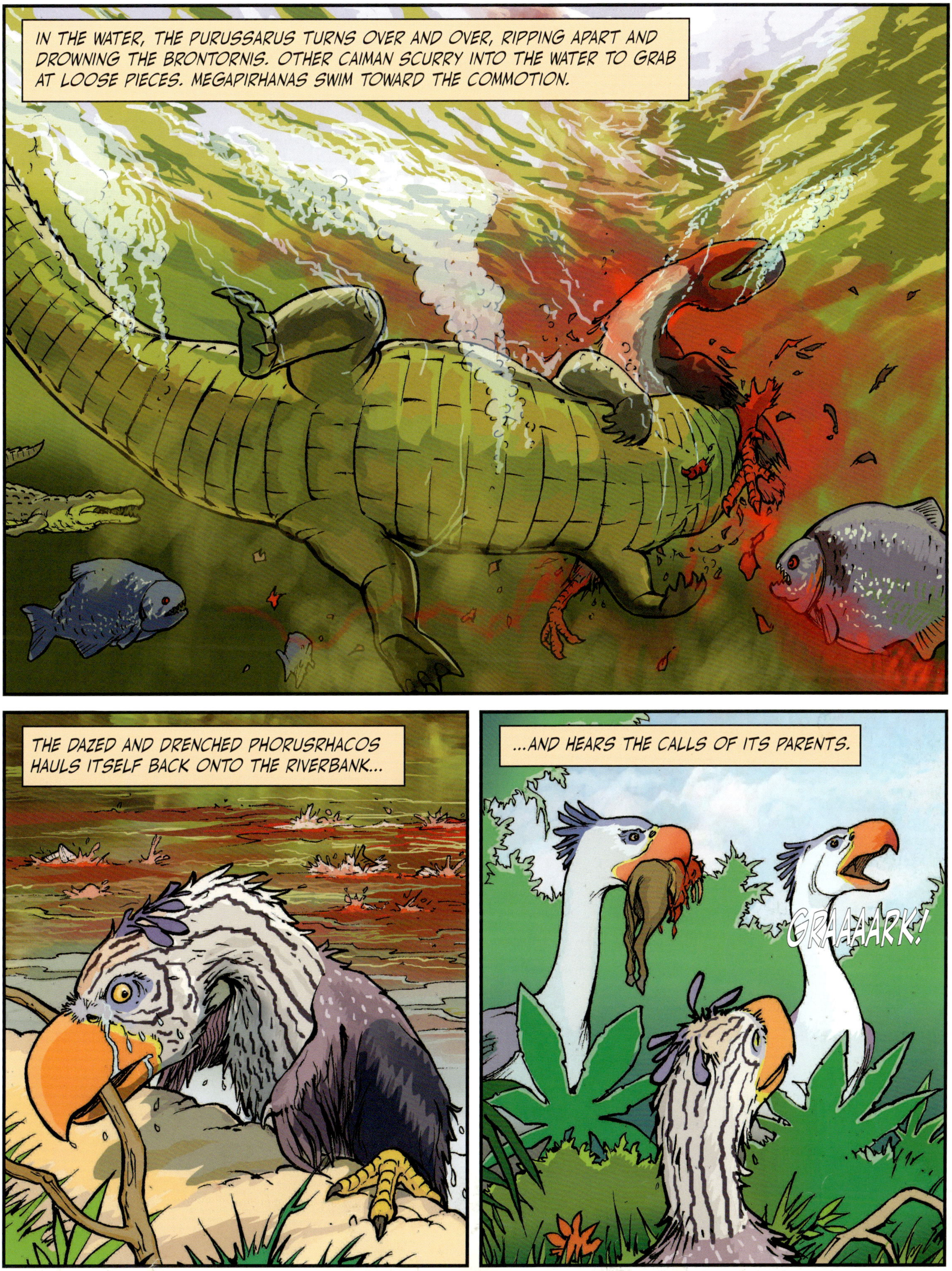
IN THE WATER, THE PURUSSARUS TURNS OVER AND OVER, RIPPING APART AND DROWNING THE BRONTORNIS. OTHER CAIMAN SCURRY INTO THE WATER TO GRAB AT LOOSE PIECES. MEGAPIRHANAS SWIM TOWARD THE COMMOTION.
THE DAZED AND DRENCHED PHORUSRHACOS HAULS ITSELF BACK ONTO THE RIVERBANK...
...AND HEARS THE CALLS OF ITS PARENTS.
GRAAAARK!

FOSSIL FINDS

WE CAN GET A GOOD IDEA OF WHAT **ANCIENT ANIMALS** MAY HAVE LOOKED LIKE FROM THEIR FOSSILS. FOSSILS ARE FORMED WHEN THE HARD PARTS OF AN ANIMAL OR PLANT BECOME BURIED AND THEN TURN TO ROCK OVER MILLIONS OF YEARS.

Four million years ago volcanoes formed a land bridge between North and South America called the **Isthmus** of Panama. Over time, animals moved between north and south. The invasion of North American predators, such as the sabertooth tiger (***Smilodon***) and bears, had a big impact on South America's prey animals. Until then, they only had the terror birds to fear. The *phorusrhacoses*, too, could not compete, and, like many of their prey, they became extinct.

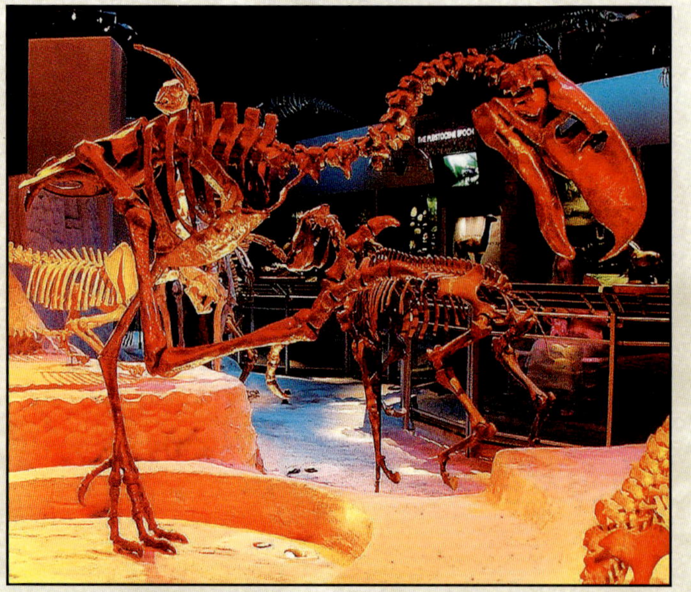

Terror birds also roamed across North America. This is a reconstructed fossil of Titanis *from fragments found in Florida.*

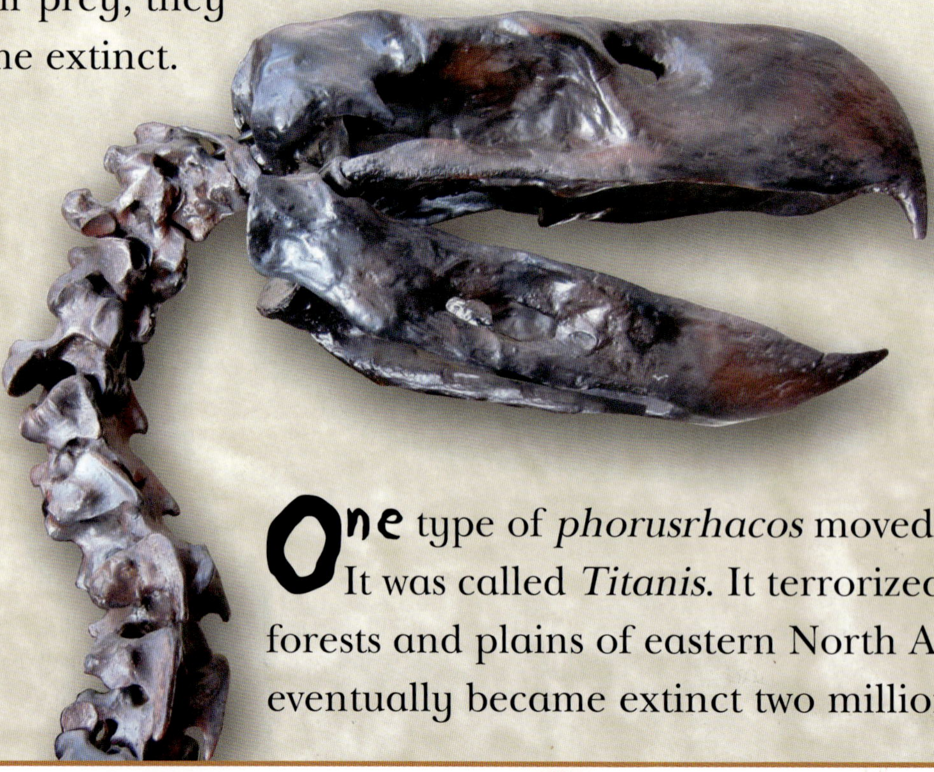

The skull of a 23 million-year-old-fossil of Paraphysornis, *a South American terror bird that stood 6.5 feet (2 m) tall.*

One type of *phorusrhacos* moved north, though. It was called *Titanis*. It terrorized the sub-tropical forests and plains of eastern North America until it eventually became extinct two million years ago.

ANIMAL GALLERY

All of these **animals** appear in the story.

tree monkey
Length: 1.4 ft (43 cm)
Although rare as fossils, small capuchin-like monkeys are known to have lived in ancient South America.

Thylacosmilus
"pouched saber"
Length: 4.5 ft (1.37 m)
a leopard-sized, sabertoothed cat with long lower jaw **flanges**, which the sabers rested on

Hapalops
Length: 3.3 ft (1 m)
a ground sloth (related to the famous giant **Megatherium**); small enough to climb trees

Macrauchenidia
"long llama"
Length: 9.8 ft (3 m)
a type of camel-like animal unique to South America that browsed and grazed; might have had a short trunk like a modern Saiga antelope

Astrapotherium
"great lightning beast"
Length: 8.2 ft (2.5 m)
a strange cross between a small elephant and a large tapir, which might have spent a lot of time in rivers browsing water plants like modern hippopotamuses do

brontornis
"thunderous bird"
Length: 9.2 ft (2.8 m)
a large, heavy type of terror bird that ambushed prey or stole others' kills

purussaurus
"dominator lizard"
Length: 39 ft (12 m)
a giant caiman (a type of alligator) that lurked in rivers to ambush prey

GLOSSARY

browsing eating mainly leaves, twigs, and nuts
clutch a pair or group of eggs that have been laid at the same time
fossil the remains of living things that have turned to rock
flanges a rim that sticks out and gives an object strength
isthmus a narrow strip of land that links two continents
lunge to thrust the body forward suddenly to attack or seize
Megatherium an ancient, elephant-sized sloth
Miocene period the time between 23,000,000 to 5,000,000 years ago, when grasslands slowly replaced global forests
Pliocene period the time between 5,000,000 and 2,000,000 years ago, just before the start of the ice ages
quarry an animal being pursued by another predatory animal
savannah grassy, almost treeless, plains in warm areas
Smilodon (Blade Tooth) was a large sabertooth cat that lived in North and South America between 2,500,000 and 10,000 years ago

INDEX

Astrapotheriums, 15, 23

Brontornises, 10, 12, 16–18, 20–21, 23
browsing, 15

fossils, 4, 22

Hapalopses, 11, 23

isthmuses, 22

Macrauchenidias, 6–10, 23
Megatheriums, 23
Miocene period, 4

Pliocene period, 4
Purussauruses, 20–21, 23

savannahs, 5

tree monkeys, 14, 23
Thylacosmiluses, 9, 13–16, 23